AUTHENTIC TRANSCRIPTIONS
WITH NOTES AND TABLATURE
Transcribed by
STEVE GORENBERG
and
KERRY O'BRIEN

ISBN 0-7935-2743-0

HAL•LEONARD™
CORPORATION
7777 W. BLUEMOUND RD. P.O. BOX 13819 MILWAUKEE, WI 53213

Copyright © 1994 by HAL LEONARD CORPORATION
International Copyright Secured   All Rights Reserved

For all works contained herein:
Unauthorized copying, arranging, adapting, recording or public performance is an infringement of copyright.
Infringers are liable under the law.

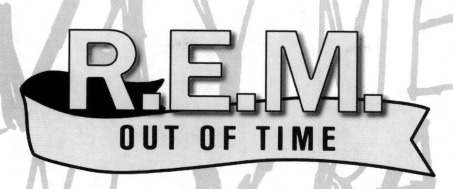

R.E.M.
OUT OF TIME

Radio Song

Words and Music by Bill Berry, Peter Buck, Mike Mills and Michael Stipe

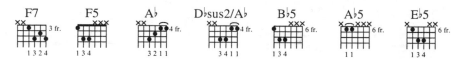

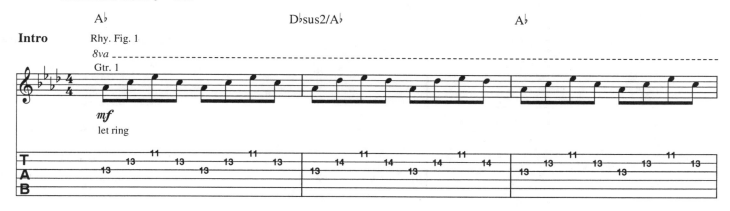

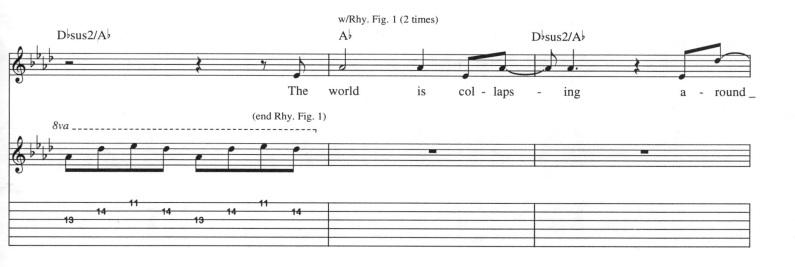

Copyright © 1991 Night Garden Music
All Rights Administered by Unichappell Music, Inc.
International Copyright Secured   All Rights Reserved

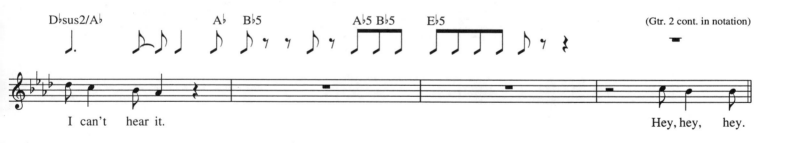

Losing My Religion

Words and Music by Bill Berry, Peter Buck, Mike Mills and Michael Stipe

Copyright © 1991 Night Garden Music
All Rights Administered by Unichappell Music, Inc.
International Copyright Secured   All Rights Reserved

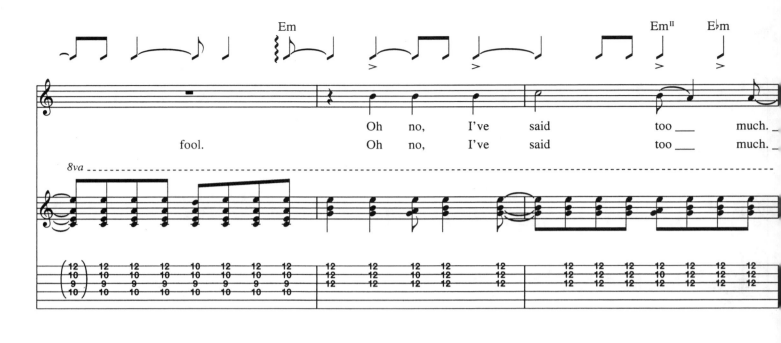

Oh no, I've said too ___ much. ___
fool.
Oh no, I've said too ___ much. ___

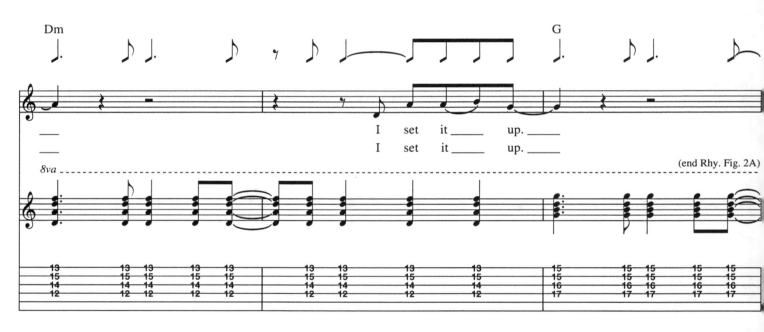

I set it ___ up. ___
I set it ___ up. ___

(end Rhy. Fig. 2A)

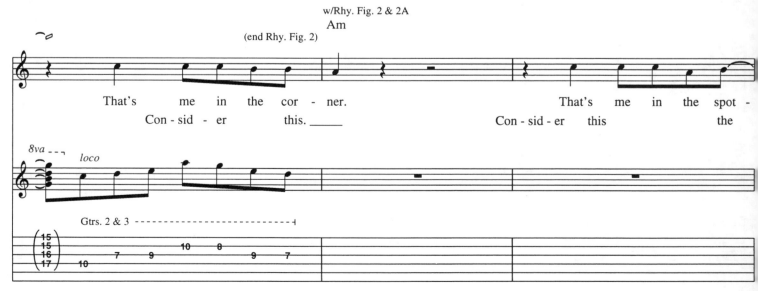

w/Rhy. Fig. 2 & 2A
Am
(end Rhy. Fig. 2)

That's me in the cor - ner.
Con - sid - er this. ___

That's me in the spot -
Con - sid - er this the

Gtrs. 2 & 3 -

Verse
w/Rhy. Figs. 2 & 2A

But that was just a dream. __

That was just a dream. ___ That's me in the cor - ner.

Gtrs. 2 & 3

That's me in the spot - light, los - ing my re - li -

gion, try - ing to keep ____ up ___ with you. __

___ and I don't ___ know if I can do it.

Oh, now I've said too ___ much. ___ I

have - n't said __ e - nough. ___ I thought that I heard you laugh -

w/Rhy. Fill 1

14

THESE FADED, BACKLIT TRANSPARENCIES REMIND PASSERSBY OF THE LIVE SPECTACLE CONTINUOUSLY TAKING PLACE ON THE INSIDE.

Low

Words and Music by Bill Berry, Peter Buck, Mike Mills and Michael Stipe

Copyright © 1991 Night Garden Music
All Rights Administered by Unichappell Music, Inc.
International Copyright Secured All Rights Reserved

Verse
w/Rhy. Fig. 1 (2 times)

Near Wild Heaven

Words and Music by Bill Berry, Peter Buck, Mike Mills and Michael Stipe

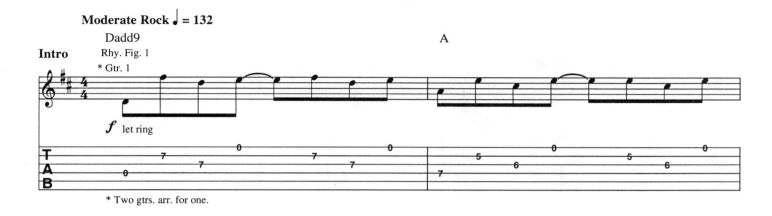

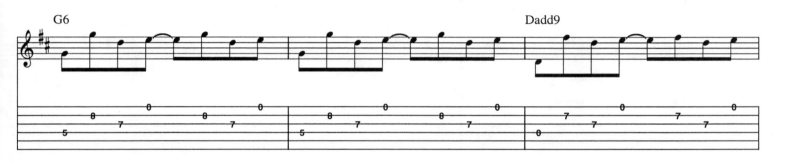

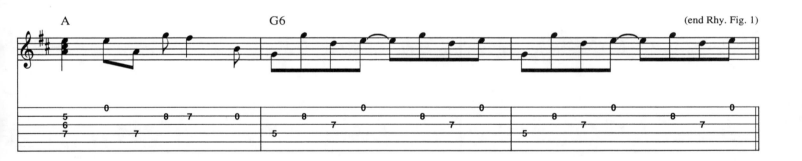

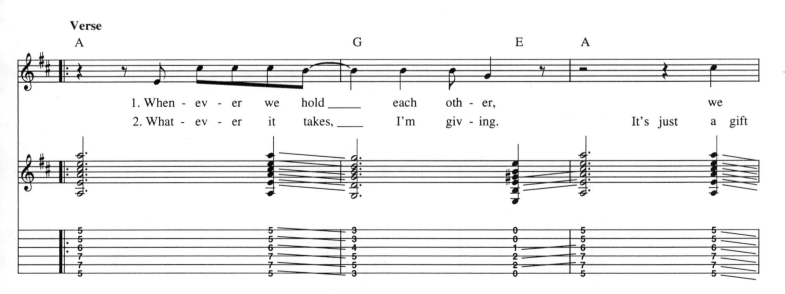

Copyright © 1991 Night Garden Music
All Rights Administered by Unichappell Music, Inc.
International Copyright Secured   All Rights Reserved

Endgame

Words and Music by Bill Berry, Peter Buck, Mike Mills and Michael Stipe

Copyright © 1991 Night Garden Music
All Rights Administered by Unichappell Music, Inc.
International Copyright Secured   All Rights Reserved

Shiny Happy People

Words and Music by Bill Berry, Peter Buck, Mike Mills and Michael Stipe

Copyright © 1991 Night Garden Music
All Rights Administered by Unichappell Music, Inc.
International Copyright Secured   All Rights Reserved

WHEN, AFTER 75
YEARS OF USE,
THE MARBLE
STEPS LEADING
INTO THE LOBBY
OF THIS BUILDING
BECOME WORN,
THEY ARE NOT
REPLACED OR
REBUILT, BUT
COVERED FOR
PROTECTION WITH
PLATES OF
CORRUGATED
IRON.

Belong

Words and Music by Bill Berry, Peter Buck, Mike Mills and Michael Stipe

Copyright © 1991 Night Garden Music
All Rights Administered by Unichappell Music, Inc.
International Copyright Secured   All Rights Reserved

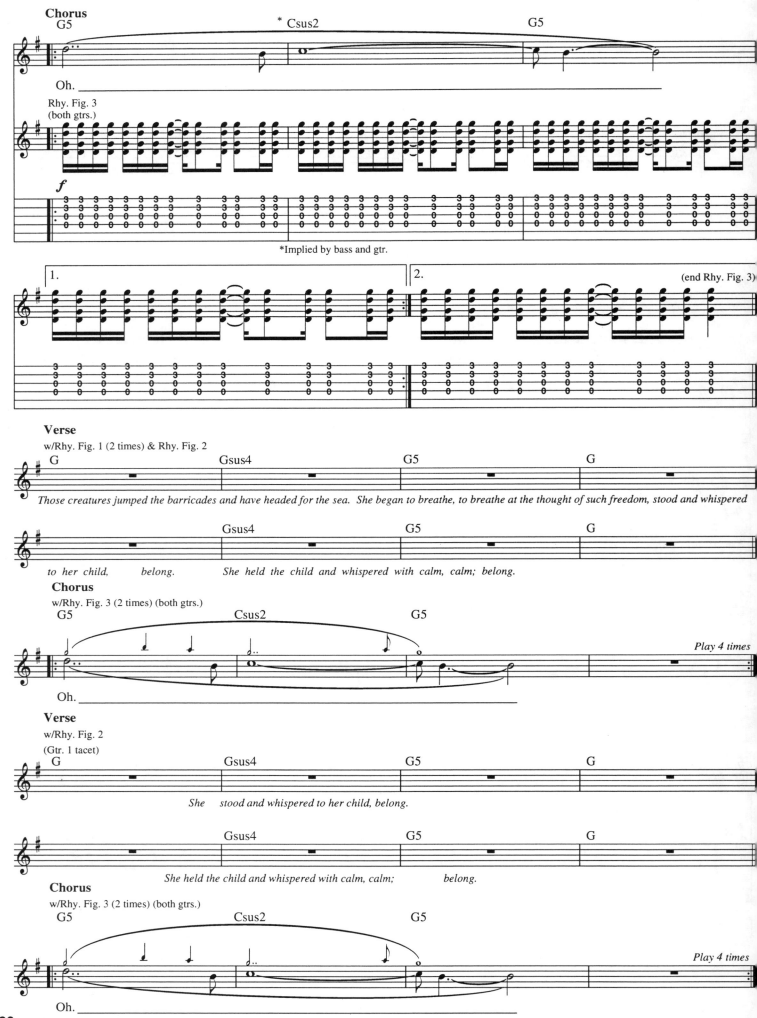

Verse

w/Rhy. Fig. 2 (Gtr. 2)

Those barricades can only hold for so long.   Her world collapsed early Sunday morning.   She took the child, held tight, opened the window;

Gtr. 1

a   breath,   this   song,   how   long, and knew,   knew;   we belong.

let ring

Chorus

w/Rhy. Fig. 3 (2 times) (both gtrs.)

Play 4 times

Oh. _____

w/Rhy. Fig. 2 (1st 4 bars - 2 times) (Gtr. 2)

Gtr. 1

Half a World Away

Words and Music by Bill Berry, Peter Buck, Mike Mills and Michael Stipe

*Mandolin arr. for gtr. Tune (low to high) : E G D A E E and place capo at 12th fret. (1st and 6th strings are not played.)
Music sounds one octave higher than written. Tab numbers are relative to capo.

Copyright © 1991 Night Garden Music
All Rights Administered by Unichappell Music, Inc.
International Copyright Secured   All Rights Reserved

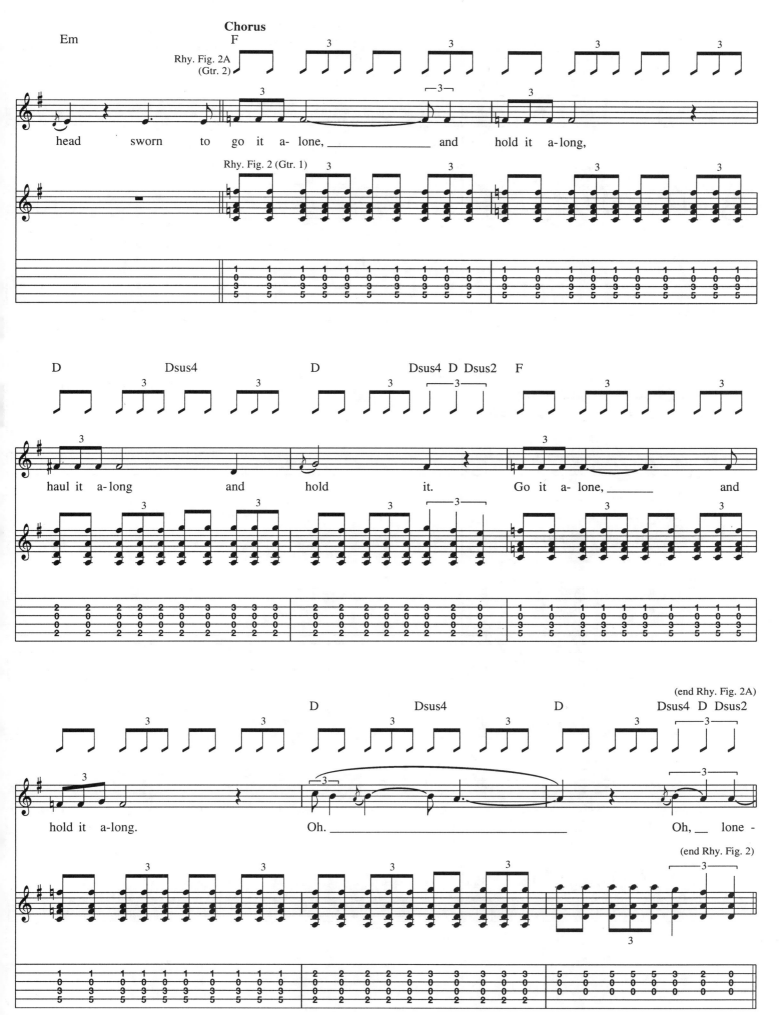

40

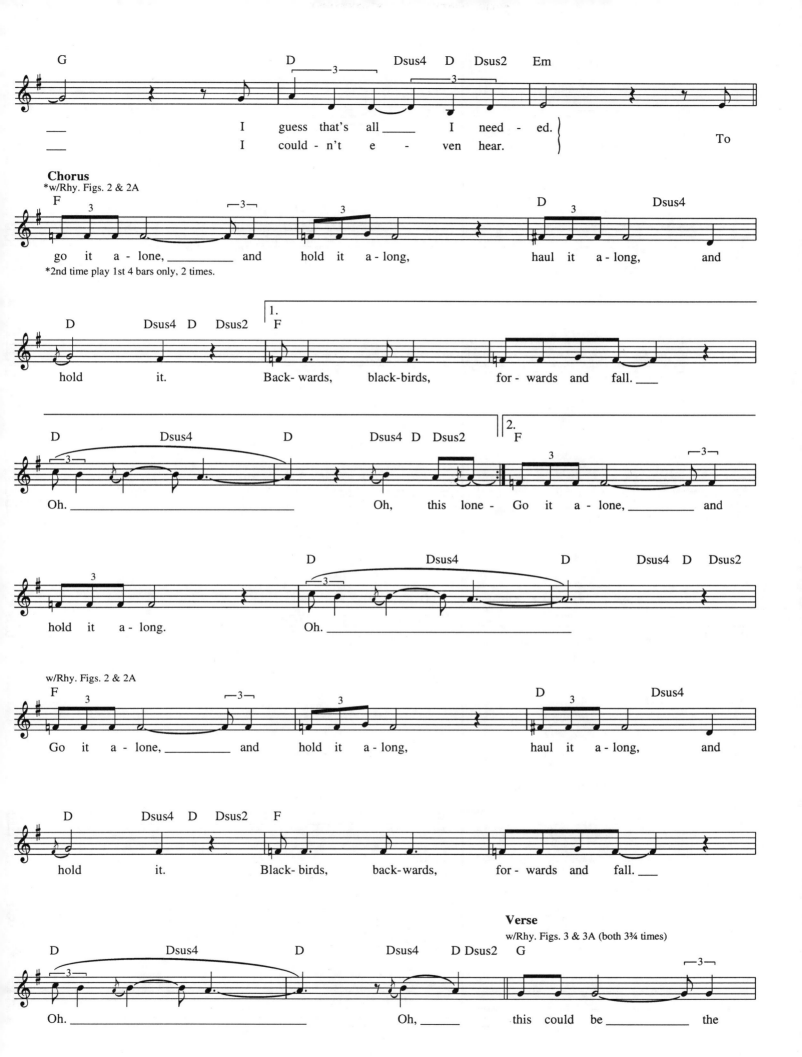

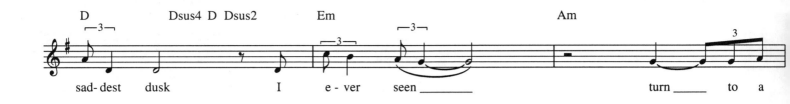

sad-dest dusk I e - ver seen _____ turn _____ to a

mir - a - cle, ___ high a - live. _____

My mind is rac - ing, as it al -

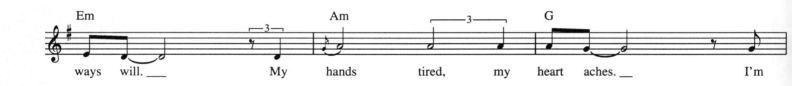

ways will. ___ My hands tired, my heart aches. __ I'm

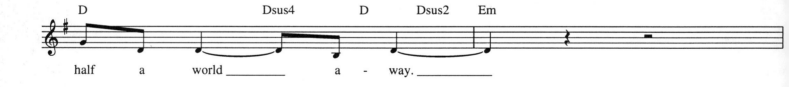

half a world _____ a - way. _____

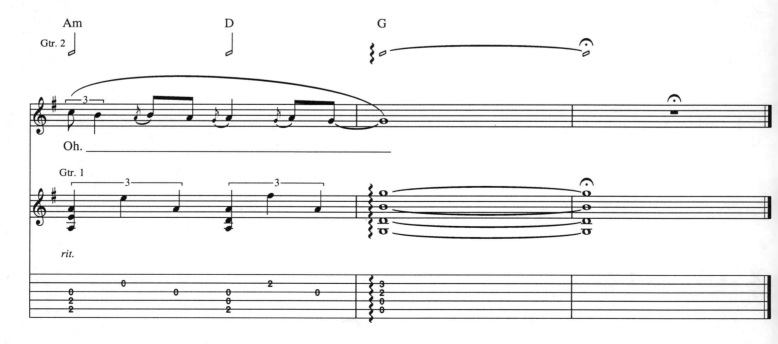

Oh. _____

Texarkana

Words and Music by Bill Berry, Peter Buck, Mike Mills and Michael Stipe

Copyright © 1991 Night Garden Music
All Rights Administered by Unichappell Music, Inc.
International Copyright Secured   All Rights Reserved

47

___ me if ____ I fall. ____

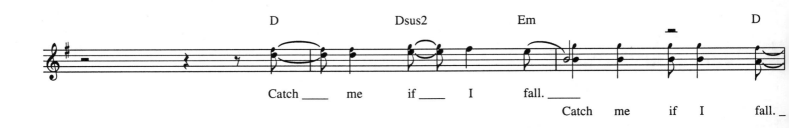

Catch ____ me if ____ I fall. ____

Catch me if I fall. _

___ Catch me if I fall. ____

Catch ____ me if ____ I fall, _

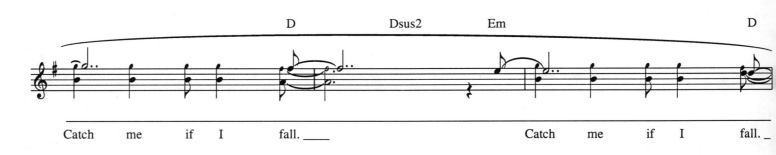

Catch me if I fall. ____

Catch me if I fall. _

Catch me if I fall. ____

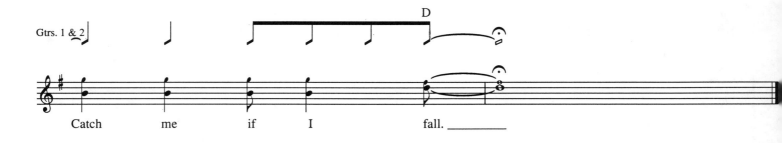

Gtrs. 1 & 2

Catch me if I fall. _____

48

Country Feedback

Words and Music by Bill Berry, Peter Buck, Mike Mills and Michael Stipe

Copyright © 1991 Night Garden Music
All Rights Administered by Unichappell Music, Inc.
International Copyright Secured   All Rights Reserved

clothes don't fit us right, _____ and I'm to blame. __ It's

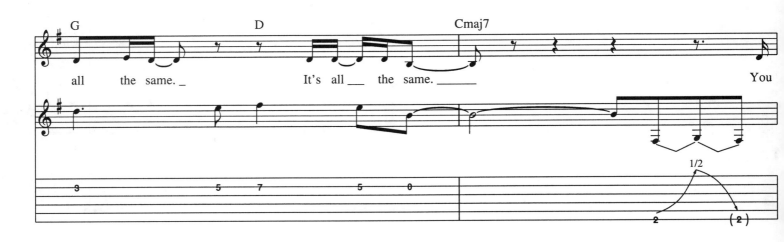

all the same. _ It's all __ the same. _____ You

come to me __ with a bone in your hand. ___ You come to me _____ with your hair _ curled tight. You

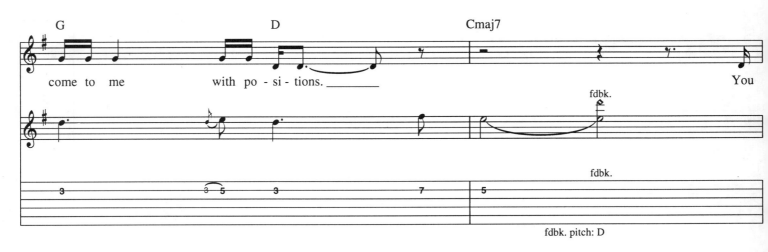

come to me with po - si - tions. _____ You

50

Me In Honey

Words and Music by Bill Berry, Peter Buck, Mike Mills and Michael Stipe

Copyright © 1991 Night Garden Music
All Rights Administered by Unichappell Music, Inc.
International Copyright Secured   All Rights Reserved

Ba-by's got some new ___ rules, ba - by said she's had it with me. ___
Got to do ___ what you do, ___ do it with me. ___
Say your piece, ___ say your sweet for me. ___
in the the hon - ey and ba - by's got a ba - by with me. ___

___ It seems a shame ___ to waste _
___ It seems a shame ___ to waste _
___ It's all the same ___ to share _
___ That's a part, ___

___ your time ___ on me. ___
___ your time ___ for me. ___
___ the pain ___ with me. ___
that's a part ___ of me. ___

Play 1st and 3rd times only

(1.) Seems a lie ___ to waste ___
(3.) It's all the same. ___ Save ___

___ your time ___ for me. ___
___ the shame ___ for me. ___

Chorus

A♭5

Left me ___ to love. ___ What it's do - ing ___ to me. ___

Rhy. Fig. 2

(end Rhy. Fig. 2)

w/Rhy. Fig. 1

D♭5

1.3.

2. There's a

NOTATION LEGEND

RECORDED VERSIONS

The Best Note-For-Note Transcriptions Availabl

ALL BOOKS INCLUDE TABLATURE

00694909 Aerosmith – Get A Grip	$19.95
00692015 Aerosmith's Greatest Hits	$18.95
00660133 Aerosmith – Pump	$18.95
00694865 Alice In Chains – Dirt	$18.95
00660225 Alice In Chains – Facelift	$18.95
00694826 Anthrax – Attack Of The Killer B's	$18.95
00660227 Anthrax – Persistence Of Time	$18.95
00694797 Armored Saint – Symbol Of Salvation	$18.95
00694876 Chet Atkins – Contemporary Styles	$18.95
00660051 Badlands	$18.95
00694880 Beatles – Abbey Road	$18.95
00694832 Beatles For Acoustic Guitar	$18.95
00660140 Beatles Guitar Book	$18.95
00694891 Beatles – Revolver	$18.95
00694863 Beatles – Sgt. Pepper's Lonely Hearts Club Band	$18.95
00694884 The Best of George Benson	$19.95
00692385 Chuck Berry	$18.95
00692200 Black Sabbath – We Sold Our Soul For Rock 'N' Roll	$18.95
00694821 Blue Heaven – Great Blues Guitar	$18.95
00694770 Jon Bon Jovi – Blaze Of Glory	$18.95
00694871 Bon Jovi – Keep The Faith	$18.95
00694774 Bon Jovi – New Jersey	$18.95
00694775 Bon Jovi – Slippery When Wet	$18.95
00694762 Cinderella – Heartbreak Station	$18.95
00692376 Cinderella – Long Cold Winter	$18.95
00692375 Cinderella – Night Songs	$18.95
00694875 Eric Clapton – Boxed Set	$75.00
00692392 Eric Clapton – Crossroads Vol. 1	$22.95
00692393 Eric Clapton – Crossroads Vol. 2	$22.95
00692394 Eric Clapton – Crossroads Vol. 3	$22.95
00660139 Eric Clapton – Journeyman	$18.95
00694869 Eric Clapton – Unplugged	$18.95
00692391 The Best of Eric Clapton	$18.95
00694896 John Mayall/Eric Clapton – Bluesbreakers	$18.95
00694873 Eric Clapton – Timepieces	$18.95
00694788 Classic Rock	$17.95
00694793 Classic Rock Instrumentals	$16.95
00694837 Albert Collins – The Complete Imperial Records	$18.95
00694862 Contemporary Country Guitar	$18.95
00660127 Alice Cooper – Trash	$18.95
00694840 Cream – Disraeli Gears	$14.95
00694844 Def Leppard – Adrenalize	$18.95
00692440 Def Leppard – High 'N' Dry/Pyromania	$18.95
00692430 Def Leppard – Hysteria	$18.95
00660186 Alex De Grassi Guitar Collection	$16.95
00694831 Derek And The Dominos – Layla & Other Assorted Love Songs	$19.95
00692240 Bo Diddley Guitar Solos	$18.95
00660175 Dio – Lock Up The Wolves	$18.95
00660178 Willie Dixon	$24.95
00694915 Electric Blues Guitar Giants	$18.95
00694852 Electric Blues Volume 1 – Book/Cassette Pack	$22.95
00694800 FireHouse	$18.95
00694867 FireHouse – Hold Your Fire	$18.95
00694894 Frank Gambale – The Great Explorers	$18.95

00694807 Danny Gatton – 88 Elmira St	$17.95
00694848 Genuine Rockabilly Guitar Hits	$19.95
00660326 Guitar Heroes	$17.95
00694780 Guitar School Classics	$17.95
00694768 Guitar School Greatest Hits	$17.95
00694854 Buddy Guy – Damn Right, I've Got The Blues	$18.95
00660325 The Harder Edge	$17.95
00694798 George Harrison Anthology	$19.95
00692930 Jimi Hendrix – Are You Experienced?	$19.95
00692931 Jimi Hendrix – Axis: Bold As Love	$19.95
00660192 The Jimi Hendrix Concerts	$24.95
00692932 Jimi Hendrix – Electric Ladyland	$24.95
00660099 Jimi Hendrix – Radio One	$24.95
00660024 Jimi Hendrix – Variations On A Theme: Red House	$18.95
00660029 Buddy Holly	$18.95
00660200 John Lee Hooker – The Healer	$18.95
00660169 John Lee Hooker – A Blues Legend	$17.95
00694850 Iron Maiden – Fear Of The Dark	$19.95
00694761 Iron Maiden – No Prayer For The Dying	$18.95
00693096 Iron Maiden – Power Slave/Somewhere In Time	$19.95
00693095 Iron Maiden	$22.95
00694833 Billy Joel For Guitar	$18.95
00660147 Eric Johnson Guitar Transcriptions	$18.95
00694799 Robert Johnson – At The Crossroads	$19.95
00693186 Judas Priest – Metal Cuts	$18.95
00660226 Judas Priest – Painkiller	$18.95
00693187 Judas Priest – Ram It Down	$18.95
00693185 Judas Priest – Vintage Hits	$18.95
00694764 Kentucky Headhunters – Pickin' On Nashville	$18.95
00694795 Kentucky Headhunters – Electric Barnyard	$18.95
00660050 B. B. King	$18.95
00694903 The Best Of Kiss	$24.95
00660068 Kix – Blow My Fuse	$18.95
00694806 L.A. Guns – Hollywood Vampires	$18.95
00694794 Best Of Los Lobos	$18.95
00660199 The Lynch Mob – Wicked Sensation	$18.95
00693412 Lynyrd Skynyrd	$18.95
00660174 Yngwie Malmsteen – Eclipse	$18.95
00694845 Yngwie Malmsteen – Fire And Ice	$18.95
00694756 Yngwie Malmsteen – Marching Out	$18.95
00694755 Yngwie Malmsteen's Rising Force	$18.95
00660001 Yngwie Malmsteen Rising Force – Odyssey	$18.95
00694757 Yngwie Malmsteen – Trilogy	$18.95
00692880 Metal Madness	$17.95
00694792 Metal Church – The Human Factor	$18.95
00660229 Monster Metal Ballads	$19.95
00694868 Gary Moore – After Hours	$18.95
00694849 Gary Moore – The Early Years	$18.95
00694802 Gary Moore – Still Got The Blues	$18.95
00694872 Vinnie Moore – Meltdown	$18.95
00694895 Nirvana – Bleach	$18.95
00694913 Nirvana – In Utero	$18.95
00694883 Nirvana – Nevermind	$18.95
00694847 Best Of Ozzy Osbourne	$22.95
00694830 Ozzy Osbourne – No More Tears	$18.95

00694855 Pearl Jam – Ten	$18.
00693800 Pink Floyd – Early Classics	$18.
00660188 Poison – Flesh & Blood	$18.
00693865 Poison – Look What The Cat Dragged In	$18.
00693864 The Best Of Police	$18.
00692535 Elvis Presley	$18.
00693910 Ratt – Invasion of Your Privacy	$18.
00693911 Ratt – Out Of The Cellar	$18.
00694892 Guitar Style Of Jerry Reed	$18.
00694899 REM – Automatic For The People	$18.
00694898 REM – Out Of Time	$18.
00660060 Robbie Robertson	$18.
00694760 Rock Classics	$17.
00693474 Rock Superstars	$17.
00694851 Rock: The 50s Volume 1 – Book/Cassette Pack	$19.
00694902 Rock: The 60s Volume 1 – Book/Cassette Pack	$24.
00694897 Roots Of Country Guitar	$19.
00694836 Richie Sambora – Stranger In This Town	$18.
00694805 Scorpions – Crazy World	$18.
00694870 Seattle Scene	$18.
00694885 Spin Doctors – Pocket Full Of Kryptonite	$18.
00694796 Steelheart	$18.
00694180 Stryper – In God We Trust	$18.
00694824 Best Of James Taylor	$14.
00694846 Testament – The Ritual	$18.
00694765 Testament – Souls Of Black	$18.
00694887 Thin Lizzy – The Best Of Thin Lizzy	$18.
00694410 The Best of U2	$18.
00694411 U2 – The Joshua Tree	$18.
00694893 Unplugged – Rock Guitar's Greatest Acoustic Hits	$18.
00660137 Steve Vai – Passion & Warfare	$24.
00694904 Vai – Sex and Religion	$19.
00694879 Stevie Ray Vaughan – In The Beginning	$18.
00660136 Stevie Ray Vaughan – In Step	$18.
00660058 Stevie Ray Vaughan – Lightnin' Blues 1983 – 1987	$22.
00694835 Stevie Ray Vaughan – The Sky Is Crying	$18.
00694776 Vaughan Brothers – Family Style	$18.
00660196 Vixen – Rev It Up	$18.
00694781 Warrant – Cherry Pie	$18.
00694787 Warrant – Dirty Rotten Filthy Stinking Rich	$18.
00694866 Warrant – Dog Eat Dog	$18.
00694789 The Muddy Waters Guitar Collection	$19.
00694888 Windham Hill Guitar Sampler	$16.
00694786 Winger	$18.
00694782 Winger – In The Heart Of The Young	$18.
00694900 Winger – Pull	$18.9

Prices and availability subject to change without notice
Some products may not be available outside the U.S.A.

FOR MORE INFORMATION, SEE YOUR LOCAL MUSIC DEALER,
OR WRITE TO:

HAL•LEONARD™
CORPORATION
7777 W. BLUEMOUND RD. P.O. BOX 13819 MILWAUKEE, WI 53213

025